STUFF EVERY
GRANDMOTHER
SHOULD KNOW

Stuff Every

Grandmother

Should Know

by Joyce Eisenberg
and Ellen Scolnic

QUIRK BOOKS

PHILADELPHIA

Library of Congress Cataloging in Publication Number: 2018943041

ISBN: 978-1-68369-098-6

Printed in China

Typeset in Adobe Garamond and Brandon Grotesque

Designed by Elissa Flanigan
Cover illustration by Molly Egan
Production management by John J. McGurk

Quirk Books
215 Church Street
Philadelphia, PA 19106
quirkbooks.com

10 9 8 7 6 5 4 3 2 1

For our grandmothers: Sophie Uberman, Pearl Kirschner, and Mary Elgart, who gave us their love of the beach and of costume jewelry and who always greeted us with a big hug and a dish of vanilla ice cream

For our children: Ben and Samantha Eisenberg and Michael, Jessica, and Andrew Scolnic, who we're counting on to make us grandmothers while we still have the energy to babysit, go to the playground, and treat them to a family vacation

BABY AND TODDLER STUFF

LITTLE KID STUFF

BIG KID STUFF AND BEYOND

Introduction

Congratulations! You're going to be a grandmother. You're already a winner. You successfully raised a child. They survived—and thrived—and now they're giving you the gift of a grandchild.

The new baby will need hugs, cuddles, food, and a clean diaper. But you already know that. So why do you need this book? Consider it a refresher—and a guide to what's changed since you were last in charge.

Read this book so that when your kids invite you to their gender reveal party, you won't be clueless. Read it for tips on where to take your grandkid for free fun when you don't want to shell out $40 for the zoo. You'll learn the rules for in-town and out-of-town grandmothers, how to survive the playground, and fifteen things you should never say.

But of all the handy, helpful advice in this book, what matters most is that you follow the parents' lead. Are they easygoing and just grateful that you bring the child back alive? Do they have strict rules about snacks and sleep schedules? Navigating your relationship with them is crucial. They are the final authority. After all, they control access to your grandchild.

Now, if this book were published fifty years ago, *parents* would likely refer to a married man and woman.

But this is the twenty-first century, and families come in all shapes, sizes, and genders. So when we say *parents*, for example, we're including everyone and anyone: single parents, couples that are married or living together, families with two mommies or two daddies. To balance inclusivity and ease of reading, we've done our best to alternate nouns and pronouns. We've also organized chapters in three stages of childhood: babies and toddlers (self-explanatory), little kids (approximately ages 3 to 10), and big kids (tweens and up).

Enjoy reading *Stuff Every Grandmother Should Know*. You'll get lots of tips, but remember to trust your instincts. There is a lot of leeway in raising a kid. After all, your own children drank water from a hose, played outside till dark without supervision, and never wore a helmet. They survived and now they've bestowed a grandchild on you.

Get ready for the journey to start all over again. But this time, you get to have all the fun and then hand the child back at the end of the day.

Grandmother
Basics

A Grandmother's Guide to Modern Child-Rearing Norms

Remember when Lucille Ball wasn't allowed to show her pregnant belly on television? Mrs. Desi Arnaz was a married woman, but she had to wear a pleated maternity blouse to hide her baby bump from her viewership. Nowadays, pregnant women are free to show off their expanding, expectant bellies. In fact, judging by celebrities' Instagram photos, showing off your pregnant belly in a bikini is practically required! Times change, and a savvy grandmother-to-be knows how to handle even the most unexpected "updates." Here are some other things about expecting a baby that have changed through the years.

"We're pregnant" proclamations. You might hear a father-to-be happily announce, "We're pregnant!" You might get updates on "our next ultrasound date" (or even "our hemorrhoids"!). Never mind that it's still the woman who bears the brunt of the stretch marks, sleepless nights, and pain of childbirth—these fathers are excited, supportive, and anxious to participate, and so such phrasing reflects the parents' attitude towards sharing responsibilities. Not all parents choose the royal *we*, but don't be shocked if they do.

Food no-nos. Once upon a time, experts maintained that an expectant mother's drinking wouldn't hurt her baby. Today, almost every bar and restaurant displays a warning sign about the risks of consuming alcohol during pregnancy. Likewise, the list of foods that could hurt a developing baby is long. Raw eggs, which may be present in eggnog, salad dressing, or cookie dough, can carry salmonella. Undercooked or raw beef or fish (this means sushi) might contain parasites. Soft cheeses, like feta and brie, are often made with unpasteurized milk, making them a risk for listeria or E. coli. Pregnant women aren't just being picky—they're following guidelines set out by the U.S. Department of Health and Human Services.

Sneak peeks. With modern medical imaging technology, you'll see more than a shadow when you "meet" your grandchild for the first time. Your child might show you a 3D-rendered ultrasound picture, or even a video, of their fetus. As the baby grows, finger, toes, facial features, and genitalia may be revealed in crystal-clear detail. The parents-to-be might even give you a recording of the baby's heartbeat.

Gender reveal parties. Thanks to prenatal testing, it's now common to know the baby's gender ahead of time. But like prom proposals, sharing the happy news has morphed beyond a mere phone call. Some couples simply post a photo of themselves online holding a sign that says, "It's a boy/girl." Others go all out and plan a party where they break the news. They might cut open a white-frosted cake to reveal a pink or blue layer, break a piñata filled with pink- or blue-wrapped candy, or set off a pink or blue smoke bomb.

Baby showers. Most expectant mothers want to be showered with gifts, but not everyone wants to celebrate prior to her due date. These days, it's best to ask the mom-to-be what she prefers, especially because some cultures and religions think a baby shower will tempt fate. In China, a party for the baby is held on the first or second full moon after the birth. In France, it's traditional to postpone gifts for the baby—and the mother—until the child's first birthday. Many expectant Jewish mothers, not wanting to attract the evil eye, don't have a baby shower, buy clothing, or decorate a nursery until after the baby is born.

Health and safety. Technology and new research are constantly improving almost every aspect of babyhood. Check out Baby Equipment Essentials (page 56), Easy Snacks for Toddlers (page 67), and Nap Time! (page 70) for how care and feeding have changed.

Gender-neutral child-rearing. More parents are eschewing the "pink for girls" and "blue for boys" rules (which haven't been around forever—in fact, in the early 1900s, things were the other way around). Unisex names like Jordan, Riley, Casey, Blake, and Skyler; girls' dresses with dinosaur graphics and rainbow swim trunks for boys; and the abolition of gender-specific aisles in the toy department in favor of grouping toys by category (action figures, vehicles, building sets, dolls, etc.) are part of a larger movement to raise children free from the constraints of traditional gender roles.

How to Pick Your Grandmother Nickname

Some women can't wait to be called Bubbe or Nonna. Others think they are too young and fashionable to ever be called Grandmother and prefer a kicky nickname like CiCi. And some grandmothers don't get much say in the matter. Here's what to expect and how to find the nickname that suits you.

You can be traditional or trendy. Although the majority of grandmothers pick old favorites like Nana, Grandmom, Grandma, and Grammy, 41 percent go by a personalized nickname, often a variation of their given name. They want something that's modern, personal, and a reflection of their personality, and fun-to-say monikers like BonBon and Zippy do the trick nicely.

The baby or toddler might name you. A babbling baby sometimes guides the choice. That's why there are so many variations of easy-to-pronounce syllables like Gigi, Mimi, BeeBee, Baba, and such. The easy combination of Nana and Grandma led one child we know to create Nama. Another, a toddler who couldn't pronounce the letter *n*, uttered his Grandmom Jean's name as Jeat, and through ten grandchildren and thirty years it stuck.

There could be a glut of grandmothers. If you are part of a stepfamily or blended family, several grandmothers might be in need of names. If two of you want to be called Grandmom, for example, you can each add your given name—Grandmom Sharon, Grandmom Kathy— to avoid confusion. Using a nickname or variation of a given name can also be a good idea for stepchildren who are reluctant to use a form of *mother* or *mom*.

Where you live might inform your choice. States in the American South, for example, have their own set of names—Big Mom, Honey, Lovey, Mawmaw, and Meemaw are all popular. In our neck of the woods around Philadelphia, you'll met many Grandmoms.

Culturally Specific Grandmother Names

A nickname from another language can be a wonderful way to reflect your heritage.

Arabic: Jida
Filipino: Lola
French: Grand-mère
German: Oma
Greek: Yiayia
Hausa: Kaka
Hebrew: Savta
Icelandic: Amma
Italian: Nonna
Japanese: Sobo or Baba
Korean: Halmoni
Russian: Babushka
Spanish: Abuela
Swahili: Bibi
Yiddish: Bubbe

Some languages distinguish between paternal and maternal grandmas. For example, in Mandarin a paternal grandmother is called Nai Nai and a maternal grandmother is Lao Lao. In Hindi it's Dadi (paternal) and Nani (maternal).

How to Be on Good Behavior

A grandchild is on the way! You're thrilled. You have so many questions and thoughts to share. But before you open your mouth, consider exercising restraint. This is your chance to practice being the kind of grandmother your child hopes you'll be: supportive and respectful. Here are some grandmother no-fly zones.

Don't suggest baby names. You might have been waiting years to have a baby named in honor or memory of a loved one, but you don't have naming rights. Resist the urge to drop obvious hints, like telling stories about how kind Uncle Morty was or how much Grandmom Jenny loved your daughter. If the prospective parents reveal a name they are considering, don't make a face or tell a story about someone you knew with that name.

Don't share their secret. If the parents-to-be are not telling others that they are pregnant, you shouldn't either. Don't blab the news, even to your best friend, and definitely keep all references, no matter how subtle, off social media. Consider yourself blessed to be in the loop and remember that it's their news to announce.

Refrain from sentences that begin like this: "When I was pregnant . . . " or "When I went into labor . . . " Remember how you didn't really talk to your kids about sex until they asked? And even then you told them only what they needed to know? The same rules apply here. Keep all birth horror stories and medical miracles to yourself.

Don't ask leading questions. If you ask the mom-to-be, "Are you going back to work?" or "Did you stock up on baby formula yet?" she will probably recognize your thinly veiled opinion. Likewise, resist the urge to email articles with titles like "Six Advantages of Living Closer to the Grandparents."

Don't disrespect your daughter-in-law. If you have questions for your daughter-in-law, ask her directly; don't make your son the go-between to find out why you weren't invited to play with the baby on Tuesday. And never complain about her to him. Think of them as a team.

When Your Family Adopts

More and more women are becoming grandmothers thanks to a son or daughter who adopts a child. However, adoption has changed dramatically over the past forty years. Records used to be sealed, and it was common for parents not to tell their children they were adopted. Today, about 65 percent of adoptions are open, meaning the biological and adoptive parents have some contact before and/or after the birth, and children are likely to know details about their biological family. These guidelines will help you prepare for the new arrival.

Be supportive. As you sort through your feelings about adoption, be positive and sensitive. This isn't an end to your family tree but a delightful new branch. Be grateful that your kid wants to have a family and appreciate the courage it took to make this decision.

Be patient. If your child or your child's partner is pregnant, you can pretty much count on when the baby will arrive. When the couple is adopting, the timeline can vary. You might not know the baby's age, gender, or arrival date. There might be delays or setbacks. Don't keep asking the parents for updates. Trust that they'll keep you informed.

Be open to many ages. Most children adopted from the United States are newborns or young infants, but children adopted from other countries are usually at least a year old, often age 2 or older. For those in foster care, the average age at adoption is 7.

Use the appropriate words. Just as you wouldn't say "my bald husband" even if it's true, don't say "my adopted grandchild." Drop the adjective. Likewise, instead of referring to the child's "real mother," say "birth mother" or "biological mother." Never comment on how different the adopted child looks from the rest of the family. Don't say "they gave her up to be adopted" but rather "they made an adoption plan." Defer to what the family says, and if you accidentally say the wrong thing, apologize and fix it in the future.

Be ready for intrusive questions. Almost 25 percent of children adopted in the U.S. were born in other countries, which means your adopted grandchild may not look like her parents. Strangers will be curious. Check with her parents to see how they want you to answer questions like, "Is she adopted?" and "Where is she from?" and then commit your answers to memory. Remember: in the end, a family's a family, and personal details are never a stranger's business.

Same-Sex Adoption

If your grandchild has two mommies or two daddies, you'll likely get even more intrusive questions. Here are some things to know before folks get nosy.

It's not uncommon. An estimated 200,000 children in the United States are being raised by a same-sex couple, according to a 2017 study by the Family Equality Council; of these, about 10 percent are adopted, which is four times the national average.

It's not unhealthy. Children's books like *Daddy, Pappa and Me* and *Heather Has Two Mommies* teach even toddlers that a family can be happy and loving no matter the gender of the parents. That sentiment is backed by data showing that these children fare just as well as those raised by opposite-sex parents in every area from academic performance to psychological health.

It's not illegal. In 2016, Supreme Court rulings made adoption by same-sex couples legal in all fifty states (although a handful of states allow faith-based adoption agencies to refuse to work with LGBTQ couples).

What to Expect on Delivery Day

Back in the day, the obstetrician did all the planning. Now couples create birth plans that spell out everything from the type of pain medications they'll accept to what music they want played in the delivery room. Though labor doesn't always go as planned, here are some things to know before the big day arrives.

- One thing that hasn't changed is that the mother-to-be will likely give birth in a hospital; less than 2 percent of births take place in a birthing center or at home. Of course, as with every aspect of child-rearing, this will depend upon the parents' wishes.

- Most couples still turn to an obstetrician to deliver their baby, but others choose a family physician or a certified nurse-midwife. Unlike the lay midwives of old, these midwives are generally registered nurses with advanced training in obstetrics and gynecology.

- Hospitals and birthing centers often allow a few support people into the delivery room, but don't assume you are one of them and invite yourself in. It's up to the new parents; after all, would you have wanted to make a guest list for the delivery room? How could you ask your best friend but not your mom? And would you want your mother-in-law to see your hoo-ha?

- The delivery room crowd might include a doula, a professional trained to offer physical and emotional support for the mother during and after childbirth. She can remind the mom-to-be to breathe during labor and teach the new parent(s) how to swaddle a baby afterward. And she won't mind bearing the brunt of all those hormone-fueled emotions—she's trained to do it.

- If the mom has a caesarean section (C-section), she'll be in an operating room, not a delivery room. In this case, she might be able to choose one person to attend the birth, and she'll likely spend several days in the hospital. Be sensitive: this is major surgery and the body needs time to heal. Plus, the mother or couple might have mixed emotions about having had a C-section rather than a vaginal delivery, especially if doing so deviated from the birth plan.

- The new parents might put crystals in the room for good vibrations, listen to a birth hypnosis app to relax, and then step into a birthing pool that's big enough for two. Just wish them good luck and hope the baby knows how to swim.

- New mothers are generally sent home within 48 hours of giving birth. So if you are invited to gaze on your grandchild, just pop in for a short visit. Give the mother privacy to feed the baby and time to rest; let the parents hold and change their newborn without an audience. Do make yourself useful in other ways: volunteer to walk the dog, stock the house with groceries, or run other essential errands.

It's Not a Competition: Dealing with the "Other" Grandmother

When your grandchild tells you that the other grandmother keeps yummy candy in her pocketbook, that's not your cue to step up your game and buy bigger, better candy to stuff in your purse. It is natural to see the other grandmother as a rival for the child's attention and affection, but it's not wise to make it a competition. (For one thing, your grandchild will pick up on it!) Here's how to start things out right.

Remember that all families are different. Grandmothers differ both in big ways, like proximity, economic status, cultural background, and personality, and in little ways, like the treats they give their grandchildren. There are no winners and losers, just different ways to show love. If your grandchild is lucky enough to have two or more grandmoms, consider it a blessing. This means he has more fans, more role models, and more unconditional love—and more babysitters for when his parents want a night out.

Don't bad-mouth the other side. Don't make fun of the birthday gift that the other grandmother gave to your grandchild. Don't ask the kids if your chocolate chip cookies are more delicious than hers or if she took them to the zoo last week. Quizzing the children puts them in an awkward position, and making someone else look bad doesn't make you look better. Try to enjoy the time you have with the grandkids and not worry about what the other half is doing.

Play well with others. If you are the only local grandparents, give the out-of-towners space and time alone with your grandkid when he comes to visit. After all, you have the geographic advantage. If you are the out-of-towner, schedule visits when you can have one-on-one time with your grandchild. If all of you live far away—or all of you are local—scheduling and planning are even more important. Some families used a shared online calendar to do this.

Coordinate holiday celebrations. Put your dibs on a particular holiday far in advance so everyone can arrange their calendars around it. Remember to take turns, and consider sharing the day or even celebrating the holiday at another time.

Make efforts to be one big happy family. Plan a barbecue or get tickets to a minor league baseball game and invite the in-laws and siblings. If you're inclusive, you'll likely be included in future gatherings.

Be on the same team when you're together. Remember being at a party in junior high where the in-crowd was huddled together talking and you felt left out? That's how the other grandmother might feel when the whole family gets together. Make an effort to include her in the conversation. Don't talk exclusively about your family's memories, old friends, or the great trip you all took. Instead, let your grandchild's parents lead the conversation. And don't try to monopolize the child's attention. There's plenty to go around.

Take turns. Try not to feel bad or insist on tagging along if your daughter tells you that the other grandparents are taking the kids out of town for the weekend. It's their time. Give them their space, and then pick a weekend for your own getaway with the kids.

Don't try to be or do everything the same. Your family's traditions, whether it's going to the beach every July or planting a vegetable garden in the spring, are special and unique, and you should share them with your grandchild. Don't get hung up on what the other half does. Focus on the things your family has always enjoyed, and your grandchild will enjoy them too.

How to Be Tech-Savvy

If you hope to stay connected with your grandchild and her parents, you need to learn or brush up on the new social networking technology. The mom-to-be will certainly have plenty on her plate, so find another expert to teach you. You can check out the adult programming at your local community center, public library or high school for a short course in "social media for seniors," but here's a crash course on various platforms and how to use them.

Video chatting: Skype, FaceTime, Facebook Messenger, and Google Duo are popular video chat apps that let you see who you are talking to. You can do this on your computer, tablet, or smartphone. Video chatting is especially fun for waving to a toddler who lives hundreds of miles away, watching her sing and dance, and generally "seeing" your grandchild grow up.

Text messaging: On average, a child gets her first smartphone around age 10 these days, and texting will be a great way for you to communicate. A text message is unobtrusive; your grandchild can see what you want and decide whether or not to answer immediately. Brush up on your emojis so you know that the red heart means love and the little pile of poop with eyes means you don't like something. Don't sign the text "Love, Grandma." She knows it's you. And if you don't get a reply right away, don't take it personally.

Instagram: Beyoncé showed off her pregnant belly on Instagram, but your daughter or daughter-in-law may not. However, she probably has an account on this photo-sharing app. You can "follow" her to see pictures of her pregnancy, vacations, and what she ordered at the restaurant last night. Tap the heart icon when you like what you see.

Pinterest: This online bulletin board lets you post pictures of things you come across online and is many people's go-to resource for planning themes, styles, and even specific purchases for big life events like weddings, parties, and (of course) babies. You can make a board labeled "My future grandchild," and when you see a rocking chair you love, click and "pin" it to the board as a reminder to pick it up before the shower. If your daughter/DIL is on Pinterest, you can ask her to share a board with you so that you can see what she likes—it's a great way to get ideas for baby nurseries, clothing, and toys.

Facebook: You probably already know that Facebook is a great way to lurk and see what your kids are up to. If you are not already your daughter or DIL's Facebook friend, ask her to friend you. You'll find out all kinds of things about her pregnancy and her life without having to ask. You can also start a family Facebook group where cousins, aunts, and siblings can connect, post old photos, leave messages, and see who else is reproducing. It's a nice place to share the good news, but do refrain from posting anything controversial.

Twitter: Twitter is a "microblogging" service that allows you to post short messages, aka "tweets," about what you're up to. Messages are limited to 280 characters (about 50 words), so this is a great place to practice editing your ideas. You can also get your news in brief, digestible nuggets. Search the hashtag #pregnancy to read tips and articles or #grandmother to follow actress Sally Field, author Anne Lamott, and other women who include grandmother among their list of accomplishments.

Social Media No-Nos

You'll want to brag about your grandchild and post photos, but don't be guilty of "sharenting," the term for parents or grandparents who share too much information online. Follow these rules.

- Don't post photos of your grandchild without her parent's permission.

- Limit Facebook posts to friends (not the public) and make your Instagram profile private.

- Don't ask personal questions publicly. When you post "Is the baby's poop still loose?" to a parent's Facebook profile, everyone can see it. Send private messages, call, or text.

- Be generous with your "likes," but not your comments. When you comment, your kids will know you've read their post and that you're keeping track of what they do. A "like" is more casual and less intrusive.

- Don't send friend requests to your children's (or grandchildren's) friends. That's just weird. If they want to connect, they will reach out.

Tips for Local Grandmothers

If you're lucky enough to live near your grandchildren, congratulations! You are in a great spot (literally) for building a loving relationship with them. Proximity to your beloved babies makes it easier for you to visit, attend milestone events, and, of course, babysit. Remember these important points to be the best grandmother next door ever.

Don't just drop in. This applies even if you knock on the door and announce, "We're not staying long!" Your daughter or son may seem genuinely happy to see you, but surprise visits are not always welcome. For example, you may not be busy on Tuesday at 5 p.m., but parents are trying to get dinner on the table and children are supposed to be settling down to finish homework. And no matter the time of day, there's always the chance you might be interrupting a family discussion, naptime, or any number of things they'd rather not share with you.

Make it a date. Most new parents agree that it's useful if they can count on your help on a predictable basis. Talk with them about what would work best for both of you. A full day? Wednesdays from 1 to 3 p.m.? Your house or theirs? If you babysit, Mom can have some time to herself, even just to shower or take a walk. As your grandchild grows, you'll need to discuss the changing logistics. Will you take him on outings? Drive him places? Do things with him at your home?

Learn the lay of the land. Your lucky locale comes with responsibility. Although you'll have lots of time with your grandchild, you can't spend every minute of it playing. Make an effort to learn about his daily activities, and you'll get brownie points for being helpful. How do you turn on their TV and find *Paw Patrol*? Does the baby love or hate the bouncy rocker? What does he eat for an afternoon snack? Children are creatures of habit; they will function better when you fit into their routine.

Pitch in . . . If you see something that obviously needs cleaning or picking up, sometimes it's better to just do the job rather than ask a million questions. It's unlikely that your child would object if you washed the breakfast dishes still sitting in the sink, took out the trash, or threw in a load of laundry. If you will be a regular visitor and want to make yourself useful, talk to your son or daughter about chores that would be OK for you to do without asking—and how they would like them done.

. . . but don't redecorate. Resist the urge to alphabetize the spice rack, put the laundry basket in a "more convenient" spot (where the parents might never find it), or reprogram the TV/DVR. It's not your home. Even if you trip over the shoes in their hallway every time you visit—because your son wants everyone to take their shoes off—leave them there.

Obey the house rules. As a local grandmom, you can easily go back and forth between your place and theirs. But that doesn't give you permission to feed your grandchild sugar cookies at 7 p.m. and then duck out when he refuses to go to bed an hour later. Yes, you get to give your grandchild back to their parents, but you have to give him back in "good condition." It's also not fair to play with him through his naptime and then return him to his parents overtired and grumpy.

Butt out. If you are present for family discussions or disputes, don't insert yourself in the debate. When the family is deciding what to have for dinner, it's better to keep quiet unless everyone wants to know what Grandmom thinks is best. It's not fair to use your grandchild as a shield: "Billy would love pizza for dinner. Wouldn't you, sweetheart?"

Grandma's Day Care

If your son or daughter has asked you to provide regular child care, know that it's a serious commitment. Everyone involved needs to decide exactly what is expected of each person. For example:

- How many days per week/month will you be sitting?

- When during the day will you be "on" as caregiver?

- What about driving with the child?

- What happens if someone gets sick—you or the grandchild?

- What happens when you want to take a vacation? Can an alternate sitter be found?

- Who pays for food/diapers/supplies purchased for use during the time your grandchild is with you?

- What happens if you find that you don't have the stamina to take care of a child?

Tips for Out-of-Town Grandmothers

If you live far from your grandchildren you will miss out on the daily give-and-take, but you will enjoy advantages when it comes to spending extended time together. Your visits are special because they are rare. Absence really does make the heart grow fonder.

You'll want to decide who visits whom, how often, and for how long, but don't make a rigid plan. See how the first few visits go and then adjust as necessary; alternating holidays might seem fair, but if the parents find taking the baby on the airplane too difficult, you may choose to go to them.

When the kids come to you

Happy parents mean an increased chance that they will visit again, sooner rather than later.

- Set up comfortable sleeping accommodations in your home or rent them a nearby hotel room. No one enjoys sleeping on a lumpy sofa bed.

- Stock your kitchen with your kids' and grand-kids' favorite foods—even if that means dropping $2.75 on a pint of almond milk.

- Plan some fun activities for the family but be flexible (and not disappointed) if naptime takes precedence.

- Expect your grandchild to open your bedroom door and climb into bed with you, even if it's 7 a.m. She's excited to be with you.

- Surprise your grandchild with a new toy you can explore together. Don't be reluctant to get down on the floor to play with her.

- Make sure your house is adequately kid-proofed: check How to Play Safe at Your Place (page 73) for tips.

When you go to them

- Plan ahead and avoid surprise visits. Out-of-town visitors (even if they're family!) can put a real strain on a family with kids. Find a time that's convenient for everyone.

- Discuss the length of the visit with your children before booking travel to be sure you don't overstay your welcome. In some cultures, grandparents visit for months at a time, especially if they live far away; in the United States, the average stay is one week. Be on the same page no matter what.

- Come bearing gifts for your grandchild, but ask what's wanted, needed, and appropriate before you buy anything.

- Be a good guest. Help with the dishes and the housework. Cook dinner for the family or offer to take everyone out. Better yet, volunteer to babysit so the parents can have a night to themselves.

- Read Tips for Local Grandmothers (page 36) for more ideas.

When you're missing your grandchild between visits

- Stay in touch with Skype or FaceTime. Even though you are miles apart, you can play games, sing songs, and read books together thanks to technology. (For more about video chatting, turn to page 32.)

- Regularly mail your grandkid stickers, a letter, or a drawing you made for her. Kids love getting mail.

- Sign up for a toy-of-the-month club or a kid-friendly subscription box service. Choose the one that fits your grandchild's age and interest, whether science, craft projects, reading, or cooking. Sure, it's an indulgence, but when she opens that box each month she'll think of you.

- If you need a grandchild fix and can't wait until the next official visit, pick a place halfway between you and your child and meet for a weekend of fun. You don't have to spring for a full-blown vacation—find a hotel with an indoor pool and a kitchenette, or book a house through a vacation rental website like Airbnb.com where you can all hang out together. Don't make an exhaustive list of local attractions to visit; the point of this get-together is to spend bonus downtime with your grandkid—and her parents. Of course, they'll be more likely to come if you foot the bill. Check out websites like Meethalfway.co, A.placebetween.us, and Whatshalfway.com to find a good meeting place as well as where to sleep and eat when you get there.

How to Set House Rules

Remember when your kids pushed back against your rules? Now they're in charge, and chances are you're going to push back against some of theirs. That's because grandmothers have an urge to indulge their grandchildren. "I'm there to spoil them and love them, not discipline them," one grandmother told us. To keep the urge in check so you don't end up with a timeout, follow these tips.

Let the parents set the tone. How strict the rules are and how much you can bend them depend on the child's parents. Some parents are easygoing and just grateful that Grandmom takes care of the children and brings them back alive. Others have strict rules about snacks, TV time, and sleep schedules and don't budge.

Consider the circumstances. An out-of-town grandmother has more leeway in spoiling the kid because visits are infrequent. But if you provide regular childcare—even one day a week—this behavior can undermine the house rules and confuse your grandchild. Discuss the rules with the parents, and agree on how much you can deviate from them.

Shh! Don't tell. Kids love secrets, and there's no harm in telling them an innocent one, such as "I'm going

to take everyone out for ice cream later. It's a secret."
Or "I don't like broccoli either. Don't tell. But I eat it
'cause it's good for me." But if they're not allowed to eat
ice cream for breakfast and you give it to them, don't
warn them not to tell Mommy. It's not a nice thing to
do, and they'll tell Mommy right away.

Reserve discipline for emergencies. When life and limb
are at risk—at the playground, crossing the street—
you must butt right in. But when the child is at your
house and you don't like her behavior, you can gently
say, "Please don't talk to me like that," but leave any
consequence or punishment to the parents. And if the
entire family is sitting at the dinner table and your
grandchild gets up and runs around like a banshee,
keep quiet. It's her parents' job to say, "Come back
and sit down now."

Grandmother Goals: Eight Glam-Moms to Inspire You

Becoming a grandma doesn't mean you have to don pearls and a cardigan set. You can still be cool! Let these ten famous "glam-moms" inspire you to put your own spin on grandmotherhood.

The Grandmother of All Artists

American folk artist Grandma Moses was, in fact, a grandmother. When she died at age 101, she had 30 grandchildren! Anna Mary Robertson Moses got her nickname because she was 78 years old when she started painting seriously. A year later, her paintings were included in a show of unknown artists at the Museum of Modern Art in New York City.

Her Royal Granny

Most of the world calls her Your Majesty, but to Princes William and Harry, Queen Elizabeth of England is Granny. But that isn't her only nickname. High-society gossip columnist Richard Kay reported that after a fall at Buckingham Palace, toddler Prince William called out for "Gary." When a member of the household asked, "Who is Gary?" the Queen responded, "I'm

Gary," and swooped in to comfort him. Wills had not yet mastered saying Granny, she explained.

The Grammy-Winner Grandma

Singer, songwriter, and celebrity chef Patti LaBelle has two Grammys—and two grandchildren, Gia and Leyla. LaBelle chose "Glamom" for her grandmother nickname, which fits nicely with her glamorous designer clothes, coiffed hair, and stylish manicured nails. But even if you request glamour, LaBelle says, it doesn't always work out; her granddaughters pronounce her name "Gamma."

The Silver Screen Star Grandma

Actress Blythe Danner is grandmom to daughter Gwyneth Paltrow's children, Apple and Moses Martin. But Blythe considers herself too young and stylish to be called Granny. As you might have noticed, the family likes unique names, so the grandkids call Danner "Lalo."

The Other Royal Grandmother

Could you tell the future King of England to stop teasing the dog and get down off the sofa? Carole Middleton, mother of Kate, Duchess of Cambridge, regularly babysits for her grandchildren, Princess Charlotte, baby Prince Louis, and Prince George, who is third in line for the throne. Grandmother Middleton raised a daughter who married a prince, so she probably knows what she's doing!

The Political Pantsuit Grandma

Name-calling is common in politics, and Hillary Clinton has been called a lot of names. But she has said that the name she likes most is Grandmother. She was unprepared for how having grandchildren is "like falling in love all over again." The former first lady and senator from New York is grandmother to her daughter Chelsea's two children, Charlotte and Aidan. The grandkids have political genes from both grandmoms; their paternal grandmother is Marjorie Margolies, a television journalist, politician, and women's rights advocate who was elected to Congress in 1992 and served for two years.

The (Almost) EGOT Grandmother

Known to a generation as Mary Poppins and Maria von Trapp, actress Julie Andrews also played the queen of Genovia in the Princess Diaries movies. When Anne Hathaway's character, an ordinary teenager, discovers she is a princess, grandmother/queen Andrews must teach her proper princess behavior and groom her to become royalty. In real life, Andrews has nine grandchildren (!) and has racked up three out of the four prestigious performing arts accolades that make up the EGOT: two Emmys, three Grammys, and one Oscar. Only the Tony eludes her . . . for now.

The Pop Queen Grandma

Fashion designer Tina Knowles is mom to singer/goddess Beyoncé and grandmother to her three children with music mogul Jay-Z: daughter Blue Ivy and twins, Rumi and Sir. Their daughter Rumi was named after a Persian poet who is Jay and Beyoncé's favorite. And Sir? "He carries himself like that. He just came out, like, Sir," Jay explained. We can only hope that Grandmother Tina kept her thoughts on unusual baby names to herself.

Ten Things No One Will Tell You About Grandmothering

When you're out to lunch with your friends who are already grandmothers, they beam with pride and tell you that grandchildren inspire boundless, unconditional love. They say that becoming a grandmother is a life-changing, awe-inspiring experience and that they wish their kids hadn't waited so long to have kids. This is what they don't tell you.

1. You will be thoroughly exhausted after a day of babysitting.

2. Admission to the zoo is $37.50 plus snacks and souvenirs.

3. You can buy felt-tip markers that don't stain or make a mess.

4. Rubble, the construction worker bulldog on *Paw Patrol*, is as popular as Elsa from *Frozen*.

5. Your grandson will raise one eyebrow and give you the stink eye just like his dad does.

6. Toddlers like to play with slime.

7. No matter how elaborate your planned arts and crafts activity is, the kids will finish it in fifteen minutes and ask what's next.

8. Always keep nonmelting candy—and a pack of wipes—in your pocketbook.

9. Your grandchild can make a huge mess in your house in six minutes.

10. No matter how much you love your grandkids, it's a huge relief to hand them back to their parents at the end of the day.

Don't Judge: Fifteen Things You Should Never Say

It's wonderful, amazing, and gratifying to watch your daughter or son raise your precious grandchild, but there will be times when you want to give your opinion on a topic that doesn't concern you to people who haven't asked you what you think. Let INYK be your mantra: It's Not Your Kid.

When you're tempted to utter any of the following sentences, walk directly into your bedroom closet and shout them at the wall. These sentences should never be uttered in public.

- What kind of crazy name is that? No one will ever be his friend if you name him that.

- She doesn't need to eat organic fruit. A little pesticide never hurt anyone.

- We didn't have car seats/seat belts/bike helmets and we survived.

- Why don't you let her just go outside and play? Do you have to watch her all the time?

- It's freezing. Doesn't he need a sweater?

- I never gave you an expensive toy/bad haircut/ piano lessons. She doesn't need it either!

- There's nothing wrong with this crib. You slept in it.

- Shouldn't he be rolling over/riding a bike/getting a job at his age?

- Isn't that shirt a little too fancy/boyish/outlandish for her?

- You spent $90 on that toy! He'll play with it once and forget it.

- You're going back to work? You don't need to. I never worked! What about the kids?

- You're not coming to our house for Christmas?! Where are you going?

- Make him at least taste the borscht/fried calamari/ asparagus.

- You loved trombone lessons. Why won't he play?

- You grew up fine without a fancy phone. She doesn't need it.

Baby and
Toddler Stuff

Baby Equipment Essentials

Stocking up on key baby gear to keep at your place will make it easier for your child to bring your grandchild to you. Imagine what a hassle it would be for them to schlep a stroller back and forth or load an awkward, heavy high chair into their car trunk every time they visit.

To keep expenses down, consider buying gently used items (with the exception of car seats). Many consignment and resale stores specialize in baby equipment for the very reason that kids often outgrow these items before they've worn out. Yard or rummage sales can be a gold mine too. Whether you choose new or used, consider investing in the following.

A place to sleep. Options range from a traditional crib to a multiuse item, like the venerable Graco Pack 'n Play, that can function as a changing table, infant napping station, and toddler play yard. Unlike a crib, these multipurpose options, sometimes called travel cribs or "playards," can be folded and stored when not in use. Newer models come with raised mattress inserts that make reaching the infant easier. See Nap Time! (page 70) for how to make your granchild's sleep space safe.

Secondhand Safety

In 2011, new federal safety standards banned cribs with drop sides because they were associated with infant suffocation, strangulation, and bruised fingers. You might remember that your children slept in this kind of crib. But then you probably also remember how many times the sides slammed down unexpectedly. And how your kids learned to climb out. You might see one of these cribs at a yard sale, but in fact it's illegal to sell it. Old cribs can't even be donated; they must be disassembled and thrown away. Always check online for safety recalls before buying any piece of used baby equipment.

A high chair. Nothing's more fun than feeding your precious grandbaby, and when she starts to eat solid foods (likely around 4 to 6 months), a high chair will make mealtime much easier. High chairs come in all shapes and price ranges. They should have a five-point harness and a fixed post so that the child can't climb or slide out.

If space is tight, consider a hook-on high chair. This compact seat hangs off the end of a table and can be stored easily. Food goes right on the table, and the seat holds the child at the correct height.

Once the child sits upright consistently and steadily (often around age 1), you could use a booster seat with safety straps. And when she is a little older and needs a few more inches to reach the table in a regular chair, you can go old-school and perch her on a phone book—if you can find one, that is!

A stroller. This is one children's accessory that hasn't changed much over the years. Sure, there are fancy baby joggers and models made for uneven sidewalks that cost hundreds of dollars, but the lightweight umbrella stroller that you remember taking on vacation still works well and still costs $20.

A car seat. If you're going to drive your grandchild anywhere, you need your own car seat. It's not recommended that you buy it used because you won't know if it's been recalled or compromised in an accident. If the seat is more than six years old, it might already be past its expiration date. (Yes, they expire; the seat's plastic shell breaks down and becomes brittle.) Ask the parents to recommend a model, then buy it and install it securely in your car. Plan to leave the car seat in place; it's a hassle to put it in and take it out.

Car Seat Guidelines

Child passenger safety rules vary from state to state, but here are the general guidelines.

- Children under age 4 must be properly secured in a car seat in the back seat of the vehicle.

- If the child is under age 2 and weighs less than 40 pounds, the car seat should face backward—it's safer.

- When the child reaches the required weight, you can turn the car seat to face forward.

- A child can move to a booster car seat when she turns 8, weighs more than 80 pounds, or is at least 57 inches tall.

- Even if your grandchild has outgrown a booster seat, have her sit in the back. The front seat is dangerous for littler passengers; airbags can deploy and cause head and neck injuries or suffocate a shorter child.

- Everyone should wear a properly fitted seat belt—including Grandma!

How to Change a Diaper

You might recall the great cloth-versus-disposable debate from when your kids were young. Although this is still a question—ask any new mom—it's not yours to answer. The type of diaper your precious grandbaby will use is yet another decision best left to his parents. If they want the baby in lumpy, organic, pure cotton diapers that leak, that's their right.

The first time you change the baby, it's a good idea to ask his parent to watch you—and be ready to have your mistakes pointed out. Are you using too much Balmex? Really, you're not supposed to shake powder on the baby's tush? How does this reusable cloth diaper cover fasten?

More diaper duty dos:

- When you need a clean diaper, you *really* need a clean diaper! Don't be caught empty-handed; keep a supply of diapers, wipes, and diaper rash cream at your place. If the parents prefer cloth, ask for a supply of clean ones, and find out what you should do with the dirties. And don't forget to swap out your stock of diapers for a larger size as the child grows. Trying to cram a toddler into a baby-sized diaper is never fun.

- If you don't have a changing table at your place, do the deed on a bed or the floor. It's tempting to change the baby on a sofa or table, but those surfaces can be too small or unstable, especially for a wriggly kiddo.

- Open and spread the clean diaper under the baby first—before you remove the dirty one. The new diaper serves as a clean pad for him to lie on, and when you take away the used diaper, the new one is already in place.

- Use wipes to clean the baby's diaper area, being sure to wipe front to back to avoid spreading bacteria.

- Keep one hand on the baby at all times while changing him. Never turn away or leave a baby in the midst of the diaper change.

- Remember that you can distract a squirmy kid by singing or talking to him. Give him a special toy/book/stuffed animal that's reserved for diaper changing time.

- Close the diaper. If the baby is wearing cloth, you'll put the diaper in a diaper cover that closes with Velcro or snaps. Don't look for diaper pins.

If the baby is in a disposable, peel back the wrapper to expose the sticky fasteners on each side and close it securely.

- If the diaper is cloth, you'll probably have to return it to the parents, even if it's stinky. That's why they invented ziplock bags. Wrap disposable diapers tightly and secure them using the tabs. Bury them deep in your kitchen garbage can or nag your partner to take them out.

- Keep a stocked diaper bag at your place for field trips. In addition to diapers and wipes, it should hold a change of clothes for your grandchild, a few toys, and nonperishable snacks. A water bottle or juice box is good to include too. Your bag doesn't have to be an official diaper bag; a roomy tote or duffel is fine.

How to Feed a Baby

Although it might have been decades since you last held a bottle and burped a baby, experienced grandmothers report that "it comes back real fast." It also helps that your child will tell you exactly how, what, and when to feed their infant. Whether you're filling the bottle with breast milk or formula, here's a refresher course.

1. **Sterilize the bottle.** Remember when you had to sterilize bottles using boiling water? You're off the hook—doctors now say boiling is unnecessary and that putting a bottle in the dishwasher or hand-washing it with hot soapy water is sufficient. Wash each bottle after every feeding and allow it to dry completely before using it again. And be sure to wash your hands before you feed the baby.

2. **Prepare the formula or breast milk.** If the baby is formula-fed, it's the parent's job to choose the formula—organic or non-GMO, low-lactose or iron-added, soy protein or goat's milk, powder, liquid concentrate, or ready-to-feed. Your job is to read the package directions. Don't assume the formula will be mixed with water using a one-to-one ratio, or that you need to add water

at all. Ask the parents to demonstrate how they make a bottle before your first time. If the baby is breastfed, Mom might collect and freeze her breast milk, which allows other people—including Grandma—to feed the baby. The milk, which is stored in small bags, can last for 4 to 6 months in the freezer.

> **NOTE:** It takes about 12 hours to thaw breast milk in the refrigerator. If you're in a rush, hold the bag under warm running tap water or put it in a bowl of warm water. Like a Thanksgiving turkey, breast milk should not be thawed at room temperature.
>
> Prep the bottle right before you need it. If the baby doesn't drink it immediately, put it in the fridge. Breast milk can be left out at room temperature for up to 4 hours.

3. **Adjust the temperature.** You might remember squirting a few drops on your wrist to check the temperature . . . and that trick still works. If the baby prefers warm milk, run the bottle under warm water. Avoid the microwave, which can create hot spots in the liquid and damage the nutrients in breast milk by heating it too high above body temperature.

4. **Feed the baby—finally.** Hold the baby in the crook of your arm halfway between sitting up and lying down. For your comfort, prop your arm on a pillow. Tilt the bottle so the nipple is full of milk, and as she drinks and the bottle slowly drains, continue to tilt it further.

5. **Burp the baby.** Most babies need to burp after a feeding to get rid of air they swallowed while eating. Drape a clean cloth over your shoulder. Then lift the baby to your shoulder, support her head and neck, and gently pat or rub her back. If she doesn't burp, don't worry. You got a good hug!

6. **Manage the leftovers.** If the baby doesn't finish the bottle of formula, discard what's left. Dumping it might feel wasteful, but bacteria from the baby's mouth can multiply in the fridge. Before you throw out breast milk, check with the parents. Although the jury's still out, individual moms and dads might agree with those experts who say breast milk's antibacterial properties make it safe for reuse.

7. **Introducing solid food.** If your grandchild is 6 months or older, she will likely be eating regular

portions of solid foods between bottle feedings. Ask her parents what she is eating these days. You'll start by spoon-feeding her cereal (rice, barley, or oat) along with pureed fruits and vegetables. But finger foods like a mound of mashed potatoes or a wedge of avocado are also popular. If the baby is feeding herself, expect a mess.

Easy Snacks for Toddlers

Stroll down the baby aisle of any supermarket and you'll be amazed at the variety of fruits, veggies, and snacks just for little ones. Sure, teething biscuits are still popular, but so are organic carrot and parsnip puffs. Aseptically packaged products that don't need refrigeration have made it easier than ever to keep child-friendly foods on hand.

Before you open the buffet, be sure to check with parents about food allergies or sensitivities their child has. They might also have guidelines about snacking that are more stringent than yours. Also ask about the child's current favorite foods. You might remember how quickly your own children's tastes changed. One day raspberry yogurt was the bomb, so you stocked up. The next week you had six cartons to get rid of because no one liked it anymore.

Keep these easy snacks on hand:

- Applesauce, pudding, and gelatin cups

- Animal crackers (in the cute little circus wagon with the string), Goldfish crackers, Cheez-Its, Ritz Bits (the tiny cracker sandwiches filled with cheese or peanut butter), and cookies

- Cheerios for little eaters; almost any breakfast cereal for older kids

- Fruit snacks and fruit leather

- Mild pasteurized cheeses, like Babybel rounds in red wax, Laughing Cow spreadable wedges, and cheese sticks

- Granola bites or breakfast bars

- Hot cereals like oatmeal or farina

- Mini muffins or other small breakfast pastries

- Banana wheels, kiwi slices, pineapple bites, and mandarin orange segments

- A few varieties of canned fruit (fresh is best, but these are good to have in a pinch)

For a treat, make a parfait with gelatin, yogurt, or fruit layered with whipped cream, crushed cookies, and/or mini chocolate chips. Serve it in a fancy dish, and it will become Grandmom's special dessert.

Foods to Avoid

Experts advise waiting to introduce certain foods to children, such as honey and strawberries. Other common foods can be choking hazards or otherwise dangerous for small children, including the following.

- Hot dogs

- Grapes, apples, and carrots

- Hard candies, mints, and gum

- Marshmallows

- Popcorn

- Peanut butter (a common allergen, but also sticky and difficult to swallow)

Nap Time! How to Help Them Get Zzzs

Babies need naps, and after a few hours of babysitting, you'll need one too. To ensure that you both get a little downtime, ask the parents how they put the baby to sleep. Better yet, watch them, because nap time has likely changed since the last time you cared for a wee one. The first difference you'll notice is that, other than the fitted sheet, the crib is empty. These days, infants do not sleep with pillows, blankets, stuffed animals, or toys. Babies sleep in a onesie or, in winter, a sleep sack or wearable blanket. You'll also notice that the infant is placed on his back, not on his stomach like you used to do. Tummy time is just for daytime.

These changes are to make sure that nothing gets in the way of the baby's breathing and to decrease the risk of sudden infant death syndrome (SIDS). Some of these restrictions ease up when the child is around 12 months old or able to roll over. Here are some pointers for sleep success whether at your house or theirs.

- Babies sleep a lot. Until they are about a year old, most babies need two daytime naps averaging thirty minutes to two hours. They generally transition to one nap a day between ages 1 and 2.

- Babies need a consistent routine, so try to keep to their sleep schedule and don't plan to go to a story hour during their regular naptime.

- That said, when your grandchild is awake, play, play, play. Floor time, when he can roll around and reach for dangling toys, tires a baby out. So does a stroll in fresh air.

- Recognize his sleepy signs—rubbing eyes, yawning, sucking his fingers, fussing. The mantra of one mother we spoke to is, "Don't miss the window of napportunity."

- Give the baby a bottle and change his diaper before you lay him down so hunger and wetness don't interrupt his sleep.

- Follow the baby's presleep routine to help him wind down. This might include dimming the lights, reading a book, singing or humming a song, and offering him a pacifier.

- Should you move a baby who has fallen asleep in his car seat or stroller to a crib? Of course a crib is best, but sometimes a nap is just a nap. Remember the expression "never wake a sleeping baby."

- Ask the parents what to do if the baby starts fussing after being asleep. Should you go in to comfort him or wait to see if he'll settle down?

- Learn how to use the parents' baby monitor, which might include an alarm, infrared night vision, and a zoom camera that you can access through an app on your smartphone.

How to Play Safe at Your Place

You might love your collection of fragile porcelain swans, but now that you're a grandmother everyone will breathe easier if the swans swim safely on a high shelf. You need to childproof.

You don't have to redesign your whole house, but do make a safe place for your grandchild to play, even if it's just a room. It will make life easier. Prioritize what's dangerous versus what could lead to a potential mess. A potted plant on the floor would require cleanup if your toddler gets into it; a heavy mirror leaning against a wall is a serious danger and must be moved. Start with these safety measures.

Take a look. Childproofing experts advise getting down on all fours and looking at your room from a child's point of view. Are cords dangling from window shades and wires extending from outlets? Is the coffee table made of glass? Shorten cords, tie wires back, and install edge guards on sharp furniture corners.

Secure heavy furniture. Children like to pull out drawers and use them as steps to climb. This is extremely dangerous and will cause the furniture to topple over. Heavy bookcases, bureaus, and televisions must be bolted or strapped to a wall. Kits to help you do this are available at major online retailers, as well as baby-centric outlets like Buy Buy Baby.

Cover the plugs. Plastic outlet covers are inexpensive and easy to use. Put them in rooms where the child plays to protect her little fingers from a jolt of electricity.

Eliminate other hazards. You'll soon learn what your grandchild likes to get into. Anything that can fit inside a cardboard toilet-paper tube can be a choking hazard. That means your open jar of pennies needs to go in a drawer with a childproof lock on it. Put another lock on your cabinet of cleaning supplies and move anything else risky to a cabinet they can't easily get into. It will be safer and more fun for all. And don't forget, you can keep toddlers out of a room by simply closing a door.

Of course, the best safety advice is to stay vigilant. Don't leave little ones alone, even for a minute.

Five Ideas for Silly, Active Toddler Fun

Toddlers love to run around. And let's face it, exercise is great for grandmothers too. Kids also like to be silly, and when you join in with enthusiasm, they like it even more. Here are five fun, lively games the two of you can play together indoors or out. Some are old-time classics—like you!

The Walking, Walking Song

Sing this song together to the tune of "Frère Jacques" as you move around in a circle. When you sing about walking, walk. When you sing about hopping, hop. And so on.

Walking, walking, walking, walking,
Hop, hop, hop! Hop, hop, hop!
Running, running, running, running,
Now we stop. Now we stop.
Repeat . . .

Sock Toss

Gather a pile of rolled-up, matched socks. (If you have unmatched socks of different colors, sort them into color piles and then make pairs of socks in the same color.) Place an empty laundry basket about 2 feet away from where you and your grandchild stand together. Show her how to toss a pair into the basket. Take turns, announcing "your turn" and "my turn." Keep score. For variety, try throwing just blue pairs. The possibilities are endless.

The Hokey-Pokey

Stand next to each other and sing the song while performing the corresponding motions. Your toddler probably won't know right from left, but she can follow your lead.

You put your right foot in,
You put your right foot out,
You put your right foot in,
And you shake it all about.
You do the Hokey-Pokey
    (raise your hands and wiggle your fingers)
And you turn yourself around
    (turn in a full circle)
That's what it's all about.

Continue with the left foot, right and left arms, and then your whole self. Don't stop there. Choose other body parts the child knows, including her hair, tongue, and backside.

Dance Contest

Put on music—one of your grandchild's favorites and then one of yours. Pull out some props, such as small scarves, ribbons, flashlights, or plastic flowers, and show off your dance moves. You can each do a solo dance or grab a doll or stuffed animal as a partner. You can also join hands and dance together.

Hide-and-Seek

Don't forget the easiest toddler favorite: having you search the whole house for her even though you can see her feet sticking out from behind the sofa. To a toddler, the game means hiding from you in plain sight, with her hands over her eyes. Your job is to take your time and look in every nook and cranny before you find her—and then act surprised. When it's your turn, hide where you can be found easily, too.

Get a Little Woo-Woo: Superstitions to Protect Your Grandbaby

Modern science and medicine do their best to keep babies safe and healthy, but you can't be too careful. That's why so many cultures around the world recognize superstitions intended to protect babies. Traditions vary but most have the same goal: to keep away demons, devils, jinxes, and curses. The most famous curse is the evil eye, which can be cast by a malevolent stare.

- **From Russia:** Don't take a picture of a baby until he is 1 month old. Someone could look at him with the evil eye and make him ill.

- **From China:** Don't dress your baby in clothes with monkey prints. It could give the baby the monkey's negative traits like stubbornness, impatience, and fussiness.

- **From Jewish custom:** Tie red ribbons or strings to the child's bedding—and underwear!—to protect him from the evil eye or Lilith, a demon who steals babies in the night.

- **From India:** Place an onion or a knife under the bed to keep away bad dreams.

- **From Newfoundland:** Put a coin in the baby carriage and bassinet so that a fairy doesn't steal the baby and replace him with a fairy child.

- **From Greece:** Don't let a new baby look at himself in a mirror or his soul will be stolen.

- **From China:** For good luck and protection, shave the baby's head when he is exactly 1 month old. Tie a lock of the hair with a red string and keep it safe, or tuck it under the baby's pillow for better sleep.

- Many cultures have a belief about safeguarding against the evil eye by not complimenting or praising the baby. In Thailand, you might hear an adult sweetly coo something like, "The baby is adorable and unpleasant." In Bulgaria, adults pretend to spit and insult the baby by saying things like "May the chickens poop on you."

Little Kid
Stuff

That Was Then, This Is Now

Wondering exactly how things have changed for kids from your generation to the next . . . and the next? Use this handy cheat sheet.

Games	
You remember:	Monopoly, Clue, and classic board games
Your kids:	played Super Mario and Pokémon on their Game Boys
Your grandkids:	play Candy Crush and Dots on their phones

Water	
You remember:	drinking from the hose at your house or a neighbor's
Your kids:	drank water from individual plastic bottles because it was "better"

Your grandkids:	refill reusable water bottles because plastic trash is bad for the environment

Pacifiers

You remember:	the debate about whether sucking on a pacifier was bad for a baby's teeth
Your kids:	had orthodontic-approved silicone pacifiers—and they were worth their weight in gold
Your grandkids:	are taught to self-soothe and suck their fingers

Dolls

You remember:	those hard-to-dress Barbies with their teeny-tiny plastic shoes

Your kids:	played with Barbies, but also Cabbage Patch Kids, Star Wars action figures, and a "priceless" collection of Beanie Babies
Your grandkids:	play with superhero action figures and American Girl dolls with historically accurate clothes and accessories

School clothes

You remember:	plaid skirts, white blouses, cardigan sweaters, knee socks, and leather shoes
Your kids:	wore jeans and sneakers. Boys wore flannel shirts and girls wore leggings.
Your grandkids:	wear anything from sports jerseys to tutus, along with gender-neutral T-shirts, board shorts, and flip-flops

Television

You remember:	only three channels! You had to get up from your chair and walk over to the TV to change the channel. You couldn't wait for Saturday morning cartoons.
Your kids:	grew up with cable and had endless choices. MTV was popular with teenagers. Nickelodeon shows like *All That* and *The Amanda Show* ruled with the school-age crowd.
Your grandkids:	can watch anything at any time thanks to DVRs and on-demand television. On their iPads in bed they watch YouTube videos of cats playing the piano and skateboarders performing tricks.

How to Make Your Place Fun

There's no better way to make your grandchild feel at home than by keeping some toys at your place just for her. Try to choose different things than what she has at home. Designate a special place in your home for her stuff—a kitchen cabinet, closet, or storage box—and that will be her first stop after she gives you a hello hug. Resist the urge to let her take home the blue giraffe with her, even if she asks. Keeping it at your place will mean she looks forward to playing with Grandmom's blue giraffe and saves you from having to constantly restock.

You will, however, need to refresh your toys and art supplies as your grandchild grows. Take your cue from the child: if she gets bored easily or finishes playing with certain toys quickly, it's time to go shopping. Keep the following on hand.

Art supplies. Old-school crayons are still a classic choice. Colored markers have improved since the days when your kids left them on the sofa and you returned to a big red stain; new varieties are washable, and some don't even show their color unless they touch special paper. Colored pencils are great for older children who want to shade and blend hues. Water-soluble acrylic paints come in a rainbow of colors in small plastic bottles. Buy a few pads of drawing paper and coloring books (despite their name, so-called adult coloring books, with geometric, floral or architectural designs, are great for kids older than age 3).

Small toys. Small toys, and toys with small parts, are dangerous for children under age 3, but these toys are ideal for kids between ages 3 and 10. They don't take up much space, and kids love them. Look for top brands like Hot Wheels, Legos, Beanie Babies, Polly Pocket, and My Little Pony. Action figures based on their favorite superheroes, from Batman to Wonder Woman, will be a hit, too. For kids older than 6, keep jigsaw puzzles, word games, crossword puzzles, Sudoku, and playing cards on hand.

Board games. Want to spark a conversation with your grandchild? Play a board game together. Younger kids can play Candy Land and Chutes and Ladders; Sorry and Connect Four are good for ages 6 and up. Classics like Scrabble, Clue, Life, Battleship, and Monopoly are great for ages 8 and older. You will have plenty of time to chat as you move your Scottie dog slooooowly around the Monopoly board. Don't forget chess, checkers, and dominos. All kids enjoy the one-on-one attention that a game requires.

Books. Start a library. Designate a low shelf or basket for your grandchild's books. Picture books are great to read aloud to kids ages 3 to 5. As they grow, move on to first readers and early chapter books that you can read together and they can practice reading to you. Get advice and recommended reading lists from your local children's librarian, or look online for resources from organizations dedicated to children's literature and literacy. Scholastic.com and TheChildrensBookReview .com offer virtual bookshelves of award-winning and popular books sorted by author, subject, and age level. MulticulturalChildrensBookDay.com has lists of books that represent a wide range of cultures, religions, and backgrounds.

How to Read with Your Grandchild

You've likely been reading to your grandchild for a few years, and there's no reason to stop now that he is beginning to read on his own. If the chance to snuggle isn't motivation enough, consider this: a child's future academic success can be predicted by the amount of time his caregivers spend reading to him. As a grandmother, you might have the luxury of time that his parents do not. Here are some tips for reading together.

- Let him see you reading. For example, sit on the sofa and read aloud to your partner, and watch your initially reluctant grandchild become eager to climb onto your lap and get in on the fun.

- Take breaks to discuss and ask open-ended questions about the story. "What's the fox looking for?" "How does the little girl feel?"

- Did you save any of your child's favorite books? Introduce your grandchild to them. There's nothing better than the classics, like *Curious George*, *Charlotte's Web*, *Charlie and the Chocolate Factory*, and *Beezus and Ramona*.

- Ask your grandchild's parents what books he is enjoying now. This way you can keep up with what's popular and buy the next title in the series.

- Take a trip to the library and let your grandchild choose what he likes. Ask who his favorite authors are. What subjects does he enjoy: sharks, planets, art, basketball? You might be surprised that there's a whole series of easy readers about comic-book heroes like the Avengers and the Super Friends (find them online).

- Bring a book with you on outings to read together while you wait for a bus, to be seated at a restaurant, for an appointment, and so on.

- Don't limit yourselves to books. Page through magazines, comic books, cookbooks and catalogs together.

Five Ways to Have Fun without Toys

It's easy to get creative with playtime if you go old-school. You might even recall projects and activities you dreamed up when your kids were young. Chances are you already have these items on hand.

Newspaper. The contents of your recycling bin are the makings of fun arts and crafts projects: Color in the comic strips. Draw a mural on large pages. Cut paper into thin strips, color or paint them, and link them together to make a paper chain. Fold newspaper into a hat, a paper airplane, or a boat (with Lego people tucked inside)—to sail in the sink or bathtub.

Water. Keep a step stool handy so the little one can easily reach the sink. Fill it with water and soap bubbles; if the sink's too deep for her to reach into, place a plastic tub or disposable pan in the sink to make a smaller basin. Give the child a sponge or dish scrubbie and let her bathe a doll or plastic animals. Plastic plates and food storage containers, stainless-steel travel mugs, and paper cups (in a pinch) are safe for water play. If your sink has a spray attachment, you've got a doll shower or a car wash.

Toilet paper. Yep, that's right. An experienced grandma who spends every Friday with her two young grandsons told us that the boys adore running through her house unraveling a roll of toilet paper. They hit on the idea by "accident," and instead of yelling or correcting the creative children, she embraced the idea. When the boys now ask if they can "play TP," they each get a roll to unravel. They make a trail through the rooms. They follow the strips like a maze and wrap each other like mummies. Then they all help gather up the paper. At 12 rolls for $5.99 it's cheap fun—and, best of all, something they aren't allowed to do at home.

Empty boxes. Kids have wild imaginations and can make a whole world from cardboard. Boxes from cereal, crackers, and online purchases can be decorated, lined up, and turned into a town for toy cars, trains, and action figures. If the box has pictures or words on the outside, wrap it with paper grocery bags and help your grandchild decorate it with markers, crayons, stickers, glitter glue, or craft paint. Kids love familiar things, so label the boxes "Mommy's office," "School," and other places from the neighborhood. For even more fun, build a box car (see opposite).

How to Make a Box Car

This project is fun for you to build together, and your grandchild will play with it for weeks. The only essential item is a box that's large enough for her to sit in.

Leaving the bottom of the box taped shut, tuck in three of the four open flaps at the top. Lift the remaining flap and tape in place to keep it upright. Then cut out the center of the flap and fasten a piece of plastic wrap across for a "real" windshield.

Make wheels out of paper plates. Use masking or colored tape to add details. Affix them to the car with glue or tape. Use another paper plate to make a steering wheel.

Inside the car, make a dashboard beneath the windshield. Glue bottle caps, squares of foil, and small boxes onto the dash as buttons and controls. Stickers make great dashboard equipment.

Draw stripes and decorations on the exterior. Old CDs make swell headlights.

Extra credit if you position the box car in front of the television and explain drive-in movies to your grandchild.

Play dough. You might not have a tub of Play-Doh on hand, but if you have flour and water you and your grandchild can make homemade modeling compound together. Many recipes are available online and in kids' activity books; this one requires a little cooking. An older child can help stir the mixture on the stove; a child of any age can help knead the dough into shape once it cools—and everyone can play with it once it comes together!

Ingredients

1 cup flour
1 cup water
½ cup salt
1 tablespoon cream of tartar
1 tablespoon cooking oil
A few drops of food coloring

Directions

Combine all of the ingredients except the food coloring in a medium saucepan. Place on the stove over medium-low heat and stir. The mixture will be lumpy. It will start to thicken quickly and come together into a dough. Remove from the heat and stir in the food coloring. Turn the dough out onto a plate or sheet of newspaper and let cool completely. Knead a few times to bring dough together.

NOTE: Cream of tartar makes the dough last longer (at least a few weeks stored in an airtight container—in the fridge if you like) without getting moldy. If you don't have it on hand, you can still use this recipe to make perfectly nice play dough. It just might get moldy in a week or so.

Five Ways to Have Fun with Food

Cooking is a fun activity that emphasizes all kinds of learning. Teach your grandchild reading and math skills as you prepare the recipe. Model behaviors like taking turns, practicing patience—the muffins need 12 more minutes!—and tasting new foods. Best of all, there's a delicious reward at the end of your project. Use these tips to get cooking.

Use a boxed mix. When you're baking for adults, you might want to whip up something from scratch, but taking the shortcut of a mix is ideal when you're making muffins, cupcakes, or brownies with kids. With your guidance, the package instructions are simple enough for most grade-schoolers to follow. Most mixes require minimal additions, such as an egg, water, and cooking oil, and tasty results are guaranteed in 30 minutes.

Stock up on sprinkles and tubes of icing. Ready-made decorations in a variety of shapes and colors are available in the supermarket's baking aisle. Craft stores have hundreds of cake decorating items. Buy a pack of sugar googly eyes and blue glitter gel, and your grandchild can make cupcakes with faces and hair!

Play with your food. Thin sandwiches—cheese slices, cream cheese, PB&J—can be cut into a circle with a drinking glass or into shapes with cookie cutters. Cut fruit into bite-sized pieces and let kids thread them on wooden skewers with mini marshmallows for fruit kabobs. Let them string a necklace of Cheerios or Froot Loops cereal (bonus points if you offer shoestring licorice instead of string). Provide kids a variety of small or cut-up foods and let them make a food face on their plates; try raisins, mini marshmallows, or cucumber wheels for eyes, green beans or pasta for hair, and mandarin oranges or bananas for a smile.

Dress up the pancakes. Let your grandchild crack the egg (into a smaller dish first, in case of broken shell pieces) and measure the water or milk. Transfer the mixed batter to a measuring cup with a spout to make it easier to pour shapes into the pan. With the batter, form her initial, a star, a snowman, or a dog with floppy ears. Teach older children how to flip the pancakes with a spatula. Sprinkle blueberries, raisins, or chocolate chips into the batter or directly onto individual pancakes in the pan (quickly, before they set).

Pump up the pasta. Look for playful shapes, such as wheels, campanelle, small shells, and orecchiette, which are all easier for little kids to eat than spaghetti. If your grandchild is older, teach him how to twirl spaghetti. Boxed macaroni-and-cheese mixes come in kid-friendly shapes including dinosaurs and cartoon characters; you can dress these up by adding fresh cheese, cooked chopped veggies, or small pieces of cooked chicken or sausage. Experiment with different sauces, too; most kids prefer a simple melted butter sauce rather than traditional tomato, but your grandkid might like pesto, alfredo, or meat sauce. You can also use pureed baby foods—squash, sweet potato, or mixed veggies—as a smooth, tasty sauce for cooked pasta.

Four Classic Cookie Recipes

Sure, not all grandmothers like to bake, but almost everyone likes cookies. Here are four tasty options to whip up and enjoy together.

Chocolate Chip Cookies
Makes 2 dozen

> 1⅓ cups all-purpose flour
> ½ teaspoon baking soda
> ½ teaspoon salt
> ½ cup unsalted butter, room temperature
> ⅓ cup granulated sugar
> ½ cup light brown sugar
> 1 egg
> ¾ teaspoon vanilla extract
> 1 cup bittersweet chocolate chips or chunks

Preheat oven to 350°F and line several cookie sheets with parchment paper. Sift flour, baking soda, and salt into a big bowl and stir to combine. Set aside.

With an electric mixer, cream butter and sugars until light and fluffy. Add egg and vanilla and mix until just combined. Add flour mixture to butter mixture. Mix on low speed until incorporated. Have your grandchild stir in chocolate chips with a wooden spoon.

Drop tablespoon-sized balls of dough about 2 inches apart onto prepared cookie sheets. Bake for 8 to 10 minutes, rotating sheets halfway through baking. Let cookies cool on sheets for a minute or two before transferring them to a rack, and be careful of little fingers near hot pans!

Old-Fashioned Sugar Cookies
Makes 2 dozen

    3 cups all-purpose flour
    1 teaspoon baking soda
    ½ teaspoon salt
    1 cup unsalted butter, room temperature
    1¾ cups granulated sugar
    ¼ cup light brown sugar
    2 eggs, beaten
    2 teaspoons vanilla extract
    Sprinkles for decorating

Preheat oven to 325°F. Line several cookie sheets with parchment paper. Sift flour, baking soda, and salt into a big bowl and whisk gently. Set aside.

With an electric mixer cream butter and sugars for several minutes, until light and fluffy. Add egg and vanilla and mix just until combined. Reduce mixer speed and add flour mixture to butter mixture in thirds.

Mix until no more flour is showing, stopping to scrape down the sides of the bowl if needed.

Wrap dough in plastic wrap and freeze or refrigerate until firm, about 20 minutes in the freezer or 45 minutes in the fridge. Break off pieces of dough and roll them quickly into 1-inch balls. Place them about 2 inches apart on prepared cookie sheets. Use your palm to slightly flatten balls.

Have your grandkid help you decorate the cookies with sprinkles. Bake for 12 to 15 minutes, or until edges start to brown, rotating sheets halfway through cooking. Let cookies cool on sheets for a minute or two before transferring them to a rack.

Oatmeal Raisin Cookies
Makes 2 dozen

½ cup unsalted butter, room temperature

⅔ cup light brown sugar

1 egg

1 teaspoon vanilla extract

¾ cup all-purpose flour

½ teaspoon baking soda

½ teaspoon salt

½ teaspoon ground cinnamon

1½ cups old-fashioned rolled oats

⅔ cup raisins

Preheat oven to 350°F. Line several cookie sheets with parchment paper. With an electric mixer cream together butter and sugar until light and fluffy. Add eggs and vanilla and mix to combine.

Into a separate bowl sift flour, baking soda, salt, and cinnamon. With mixer on low, add flour mixture to butter mixture just until incorporated. Help your grandchild stir in oats and raisins.

Scoop tablespoon-sized balls of dough about 2 inches apart onto prepared cookie sheets. Bake for 12 to 14 minutes, rotating cookie sheets halfway through baking. Let cool and enjoy.

Snickerdoodles
Makes 2 dozen

   1⅓ cups all-purpose flour
   ½ teaspoon cream of tartar
   ½ teaspoon baking soda
   ⅛ teaspoon salt
   ½ cup unsalted butter, room temperature
   ¾ cup plus 2 tablespoons granulated sugar, divided
   2 tablespoons light brown sugar
   1 egg
   1 teaspoon vanilla extract
   4 teaspoons ground cinnamon

Preheat oven to 350°F. Line several cookie sheets with parchment paper. Sift flour, cream of tartar, baking soda, and salt into a bowl; set aside. With an electric mixer cream butter, all but ¼ cup granulated sugar, and brown sugar until light and fluffy. Add egg and vanilla and mix to combine. Add flour mixture in two batches. Stop mixer when the second batch is fully combined.

In a small bowl combine the reserved sugar and cinnamon. Help your grandkid form 1-inch balls of dough and then roll them in cinnamon sugar. Place them about 2 inches apart on prepared cookie sheets and flatten slightly with your palm.

Bake for 9 to 10 minutes for chewy cookies, or 12 to 13 minutes for crispy. Place sheets on wire racks to cool for a few minutes, then transfer cookies to racks to finish cooling.

How to Survive the Playground

You've made your house safe for your grandchild, but the playground is a whole new world. Now you're responsible for her safety outdoors, and it's been a long time since you had a five-year-old. Can she really climb a rope ladder? Will she throw up if you push her too fast on the merry-go-round? Kids vary greatly in their skills and fear—or lack thereof. Remember these ground rules.

Watch the parents. Make your first playground trip of each season a family one. Go with your grandchild and one of her parents. How high does she climb? How high does she swing? Do her parents catch her at the bottom of the slide? Observe what they do and how they do it. Ask all your questions.

Be prepared. The child should wear long pants and closed shoes. Before you leave home, apply sunscreen. Pack a small light bag with Band-Aids, antiseptic cream, disinfectant wipes, bottled water, a few snacks, and your cell phone.

Dress appropriately. Of course, you'll bundle up if it's freezing, but on balmier days dress in layers so your grandchild isn't roasting after working up a sweat on the monkey bars.

Choose sides. Many playgrounds have a separate area for younger children (ages 2 to 5) with small steps, lower slides, crawl tunnels, and spring rockers. The section for school-age kids is where you'll find the horizontal bars, tall slides, and climbing equipment. Read the signs or observe the age of the kids playing in a given area and choose accordingly for your grandchild.

Keep watch. That cell phone we mentioned? It's for emergencies only. Leave it in your bag and keep an eye on your grandchild at all times. Stay close and offer a hand if necessary. This means you will not be sitting down while she is playing. And don't let her wander off or use the restroom alone.

Take turns. You're pushing the swing and your grandchild is begging you not to stop. But don't hog the swing if kids are lined up for their turn. If it's your grandchild who's been waiting, you can politely ask if the child is almost done. As much as you may be tempted, don't discipline another child or tell him it's time to get off the slide. It's up to his parents to teach him playground etiquette.

Be a good sharer. If you bring a toy to the playground, make sure it is inexpensive, expendable, and labeled with the child's name. And if she wants to play with a toy truck that's unattended, ask the other adults first: "Hey, is this anyone's? Can my granddaughter play with it?" If she is eating a snack and another child asks for some, do not automatically hand it over. You must ask their parent first before sharing food, especially in case of allergies.

Fun in the Hood: Seven Ideas for Inexpensive Activities

When you don't want to fight the crowds at the zoo or shell out big bucks for the science museum, stick closer to home; your neighborhood is chock-full of fascinating stuff that is free or low cost.

Visit a construction site. Trucks and dirt and noise, oh my! Find a safe place on the sidelines to watch the commotion, and chances are your grandchild will be captivated. Before you set out, buy a yellow plastic child's construction helmet for her and download a cheat sheet or borrow a children's book from the library to study so you both can tell the difference between a bulldozer and a backhoe.

Attend a story hour. Many public libraries and bookstores offer story times for children; ages and times are often posted on their websites. Even if you read a lot together at home, a story hour expands your grandchild's reading world. He gets to sit with other children and hear another adult reading aloud; you might be introduced to a great children's author you didn't know. Often programs include songs, nursery rhymes, puppets, or crafts. Even when it's not story time, the library and bookstore are still great stops;

the children's section likely has inviting reading nooks, child-sized tables and chairs, and games and puzzles.

Stop by your local firehouse. When they're not out saving lives, firefighters are happy to welcome kids to visit and scope out the equipment. They will probably let your grandchild climb into one of the fire engines. If it's an older station, there might even be a fire pole. Fire stations often keep a stock of stickers and coloring books to hand out. Come with a thank-you for the firefighters—cookies or brownies will be much appreciated. If you bake them with your grandchild in advance (see page 99), you'll have a full day's activity.

Wander through a plant nursery or garden store. Smell the herbs, feel the leaves, and touch the cacti—carefully. Hunt for flowers of a certain color. Let the child choose a small plant that you'll keep on your windowsill for him to water and watch when he visits, or plant it together in your garden. Buy seeds to sprout at your house; radishes, basil, marigolds, and green beans are all quick growers. Plant the seeds around the edges of a clear plastic cup and you two can watch the roots take hold and the plant sprout up.

Go to the supermarket. Instead of food shopping, make a short list of things your grandchild likes and hunt together through the store to find them. Some markets have carts for children that look like cars, free cookies at the bakery counter, and a tank of live lobsters (just don't explain their fate!).

Check out the pet store. Tell the child before you go that you won't be bringing a pet home—you are just visiting the pets like he is visiting Grandma today. A pet store is a free zoo where you can see fish, hamsters, lizards, bunnies, kittens, and more. Invite your grandchild to bring his favorite stuffed animal to the store to meet the other pets.

Stop at the frozen yogurt shop. Many shops sell yogurt by the ounce. You and your grandchild can choose your flavors, gently lower the handle to let the yogurt flow, and pick from dozens of toppings—sprinkles, syrups, candy, and more. A word of caution: even if you intend to get just a little bit, the cup fills up quickly. And though this is a treat for the kid, it's also one for you. You've been an awesome grandmother today!

Membership Has Its Benefits

When you are standing at the museum's admission booth stunned at the cost of a one-time visit for you and your grandchild, a membership seems like a great deal. But do the math before you commit. A membership is often a great deal if you plan to make one or more additional visits, and there may be other worthy perks.

While other people are waiting in line, you can flash your membership card and stroll right in. Along with the price of admission, you'll likely get discounts in the restaurants, parking garage, and gift shop—the last of which is priceless when you have a grandchild in tow. Other benefits may include free or discounted tickets to special events, behind-the-scenes tours, extended hours, and the chance to see a new exhibit before it opens to the public.

Other things to consider:

- Before you go anywhere, find out if your grandchild's parents have a family membership and if you can use it.

- If you're a senior, ask if there's a special price for older patrons. (You can also investigate discounts from your credit card company, AAA, and the like.)

- Many museums and zoos offer reciprocal memberships, which means if you buy a Philadelphia Zoo membership, you can get 50 percent off admission to more than one hundred zoos around the country.

- Public libraries often partner with local museums and arboretums to offer free family passes for a one-time visit to library cardholders. Call or go online to see what's available.

- When your membership expires, think about changing it up. Choose a different museum, garden, or zoo and introduce your grandchild—and yourself—to a new adventure.

Sightseeing Bucket List

For the kids who want to see it all, here's a list of field trips to take together.

- ☐ Public library
- ☐ Fire house
- ☐ Zoo and/or aquarium
- ☐ Botanical garden/nature preserve
- ☐ Children's museum
- ☐ Natural history museum
- ☐ Art museum
- ☐ Local landmarks
- ☐ City hall
- ☐ Amusement park/county fair
- ☐ Bowling alley

Big Kid Stuff
and Beyond

How to Learn from Your Grandkids

Kids love to be the expert. When they know something you don't, they're thrilled to explain it. Just ask them to put a new song on your phone. They'll be all over it! If you plan outings that cater to your grandchild's interests, he'll be excited to spend time with you and show you the ropes. Let an older child research and pick the activity. With a tween you might have to brainstorm the choices. Have fun on these excursions.

For the foodie

Think of how many times you've said, "Here's the children's menu. Hot dog or grilled cheese?" On this adventure, take your grandchild to a restaurant to sample a new-to-you cuisine, such as Korean, Moroccan, or Indian. Read the menu together and let him choose the food. Remember how many times you implored him to "just taste it"? Now it's your turn to sample the mango lassi shake or the bibimbap.

For the music lover

Find out what types of music your grandchild likes (if he says Euro pop, know that he's not talking about a

German soda) and find a concert that interests him—in your price range. Pop stars command sky-high prices at large arenas, but indie bands might perform for free at a local park. Check out universities and music schools for jazz and classical concerts with affordable tickets.

For the sports enthusiast

Get tickets to his favorite sporting event and let him explain to you why the point guard is running up court. You don't have to go to a stadium with 50,000 rowdy fans; see if a minor league team plays in your area. Or attend a game at a local college, especially if your grandchild is passionate about a sport that doesn't have a professional team, like field hockey, tennis, or wrestling. It's fun for a middle-schooler to watch college athletes compete in his sport—and may be a preview of his future.

For the nature lover

Take a day trip to the beach or mountains. Buy him binoculars and go bird-watching. Start a birding life list to track all the species you identify. Go rock climbing; you can watch and cheer him on (or join in, if you're feeling spry). Visit a nearby state park and listen to a ranger presentation about animals and flora in that ecosystem. Learn about plants together at a commercial greenhouse, local college botanical garden, or arboretum.

For the adventurer

For a grandchild who isn't old enough to drive a real car, the chance to drive a bumper car or go-kart is a dream come true. You can race right alongside your grandchild. Just think of your cool rating: a grandmother who goes kart racing is definitely hip/lit/off the chain. Another option is an "escape room"; at these attractions you'll pay to be locked in a room with a group of 6 or 8 people and then have 60 minutes to find clues and solve puzzles in order to escape. Rooms are themed, so you might relate better to "Back to the '70s" than to "Prison Break."

For the artist

Checking out an art museum together is an obvious choice, but how about visiting a fabric store to purchase buttons, ribbon, and fabric for a new project? Build something together like a birdhouse, bookshelf, or other piece of small furniture. Buy a dollhouse online or at a craft store, and you and your grandchild can spend years painting the walls; making curtains, rugs, and furniture; and arranging the pieces. Visit a paint-your-own pottery or sip-and-paint studio (for a daytime, all-ages, no-wine session!) and create a masterpiece together.

For the scientist

Chances are you'll find a science or natural history museum within driving distance of your home. Let your grandchild lead the way to exhibits that spark his interest, whether it's space travel, static electricity, or tornados. Then visit the gift shop, which will be stocked with kits and models you won't find anywhere else. You can take one home and work on it together. Even if you don't visit a museum, it's easy to find science projects you can do together. Get a book from the library or search online. You can build a potato clock, explode a baking soda volcano, or make slime, to name three classic projects. If you don't mind a mess and want to be the coolest grandmom ever, take out a dozen eggs and google "egg drop." You'll be making shell-saving contraptions together in no time.

How to Make Old-School Cool

Remember the thrill of taking a Polaroid picture and watching the image appear right before your eyes? Polaroids are back—because everything old eventually becomes new again if you hang around long enough. You remember the old-school versions of these current trends, which gives you the chance to be cool and to impart your coolness onto your grandchild.

Vinyl records. Still have your old Beatles albums stashed in the attic? Bring 'em out. Or buy new and classic albums—and a "vintage-inspired" turntable to play them on—at Target or Walmart. Introduce your grandchild to your favorite artists and listen to hers.

Cooking from scratch. When food gurus talk about "farm to table" and "slow food," they are speaking about using fresh ingredients and cooking from scratch, aka what you did for thirty years when you made meatloaf and mashed potatoes! Teach your grandchild how to cook your signature dish. Show her how to bake a sourdough loaf or make ravioli from scratch. Can tomatoes together. Pick your own peaches or strawberries and make preserves.

Handcrafts. Thanks to websites like Etsy.com, handcrafts are back in style. Remember making a macramé plant hanger in your college dorm? Now when you knot those cords you are crafting bohemian fiber art. If you knit, crochet, quilt, or needlepoint, you've got a skill you can share. Teach her the basics and then make projects side by side while you chat, chill, and listen to your LPs.

Pinball machines. Were you a pinball wizard in your youth? Introduce your grandchild to the silver flippers and flashing lights. Arcades are lined with vintage machines, and having a competition with your grandchild is a perfect way to pass a rainy afternoon. Bring plenty of change; some newer games cost more than a quarter.

Thrift stores. Vintage is chic, and thrift stores are more popular than ever. Take your grandchild shopping and help her find some hidden gems. Give her the history behind disco jumpsuits, Depression glass, and antique globes. (You can even point out Yugoslavia on the map!) And you might find something you want to buy too.

Sewing. If your grandchild loves *Project Runway*, you can teach her how to use your old sewing machine to make her own fashions. Find patterns in stores (or online—many hip fashion bloggers sell their own designs as printable PDFs) and browse for fabrics together. Hand sewing is useful, too: everyone should know how to reattach a button or hem a pair of pants. (But if your granddaughter's jeans are ripped around the knees, don't suggest that she sews them up—ripped jeans are all over Instagram now.)

Card games. Your grandchild might know go fish and war, but she probably doesn't know the games you played around the kitchen table with your cousins. Grab your deck of cards from the junk drawer and deal out for an instructional round of gin rummy, poker, or pinochle. If you don't have chips, play for pennies or M&Ms. If she masters cards, you can introduce her to mah-jongg, the quintessential grandmother game.

How to Cheer Them On

You're undoubtedly your grandchild's biggest fan. When he's little, you'll clap and cheer when he puts on a show in the living room. When he's older, your enthusiasm—and his performances—will go public as he takes up music, sports, dance, and so on. Here's how to support him from the sidelines.

Get an invitation. Express interest in watching your grandchild perform, and ask his parents to keep you in the loop. Don't be shy about sampling all his different activities, whether it's a jazz band concert, hip-hop dance class, or fencing match. Watching your grandchild at play gives you a new way to connect with and support him. It can also open your world—after all, when was the last time you watched a robotics competition or wrestling match?

Show up. Attend as many events as you want to, but don't add to the family's workload by expecting to be chauffeured. Take public transit, call an Uber, drive on your own, or, best of all, offer to provide transportation for others. If you're attending an outdoor sporting event, bring a folding chair and bottle of water.

Understand that times have changed. Back in the day, you played outside with your friends after school or danced in the rec room. Nowadays budding ballet dancers rehearse four days a week. Future sports stars play year-round on travel teams. In short, kids' activities can be competitive and intense, so keep that in mind when you attend.

Control your critique. Don't yell at the coach or referee if you disagree with a decision. At the school concert, don't whisper that the girl in the purple dress in the third row is singing off-key. Her mother might be sitting right in front of you. Most important of all, don't offer constructive criticism to your grandchild. It probably won't be well received—and besides, he has a coach/instructor/sensei to do that.

Keep a lid on it. Remember how you used to embarrass your children just by breathing? Well, it's easy to embarrass a grandchild, too. Don't stand up during sports practice and whoop when he makes a free throw. Don't be the person who claps between movements of the concerto. Feel free to cheer, but not so loudly that your grandchild can pick out your voice.

Document the (appropriate) moment. Don't miss the game because you're fiddling with your phone (and definitely don't be the one firing your camera flash in the darkened auditorium!). Save the photo op for after the event, showing your grandchild with medal, ribbon, or bouquet in hand.

Be a superfan. Without drawing attention to yourself, you can be the president of your grandchild's fan club. At the end of the jazz band concert, ask him to autograph the program. Bring flowers to the dance recital. Take photos of your Little Leaguer in uniform, posed with his bat and ball. When you hug him goodbye, let him know you can't wait to come to the next event.

Honor his feelings. If your grandchild expresses disappointment—his team lost the debate; he didn't stick the landing at the gymnastics meet—be empathic. Say you understand and let him know you heard him. Avoid sentences that begin, "When I was a child . . . " or "It's not whether you win or lose . . . " In fact, experts say that the best thing to say is "I love watching you play," which translates as "I love you—win or lose."

How to Be Someone They Can Talk To

When parents give unwelcome advice, their children may roll their eyes. But as a grandmother, you might have some leeway. In fact, many young people we interviewed told us they were eager for words of wisdom from their grandmothers. Here are pointers for being a confidante.

Show that you're interested. To get the talking started, routinely ask open-ended questions. "What did you do in history class today?" is more effective than "How was school?" Questions that start with *why* can put a child on the defensive. Remember the old trick of asking your child questions when you were driving together in the car? Looking ahead, rather than at each other, can open the floodgate.

Be a good listener. If you listen without judgment and lend a sympathetic ear, your grandchild might open up and share her feelings about school, friends, siblings, and even her parents' expectations. If you simply listen, she can hear herself talk out loud, and that might be all she needs to get some distance from—and ultimately solve—her problem.

Ask permission. Ask if she wants advice before you dole it out. If she gives the go-ahead, don't worry about trying to figure out all the nuances of modern teenagerhood; acknowledge that you don't know what it's like to be a 14-year-old in today's world, but also share your own experience and the lessons you learned in similar situations. Your advice will probably bridge the generation gap.

Don't take sides. As the grandmother, you'll likely be perceived as neutral and trusted by both the parent and child—unless you blow it. If your granddaughter complains that she got in trouble because she stayed out beyond curfew and didn't call home, don't lecture her. Her parents have probably done plenty of that. Instead, point out the bigger picture: yes, curfew is arbitrary, but parents have rules for her safety and they can't help but worry.

Don't violate her confidence. Never tell Mom and Dad or your friends what your grandchild told you in privacy. Whether it's good news or bad, it's hers to share. If she has an issue that needs to be addressed, help her think of possible solutions—maybe she needs to have a conversation with the person involved. However, if the situation is potentially dangerous, or if she has been engaging in risky behavior (think drugs, binge drinking, or unsafe sex), tell her that you'll always support her but insist that she speak to a parent (or a trusted teacher, counselor, or faith leader) so that she doesn't get hurt.

Conversation Starters

When there's a lull in the conversation, you can get the ball rolling by asking questions. Share something personal about yourself first and then ask a question. For example, talk about your best friend in fourth grade and how you'd walk home from school with her, and then ask your grandchild about her best friend. Other questions to ask:

Who do you sit with at lunch?

What do you do at recess?

What book are you reading now?

What do you wish you could learn at school?

What kind of TV shows do you like?

If you could solve one problem in the world, what would it be?

What would you do on your perfect day?

What do you like most about yourself?

If you won a million dollars, what would you do with it?

What subject would be the most fun to teach?

How to Treat Them (and Treat Them Right)

Nothing says love like an ice cream cone, and treating your grandchild to a tasty frozen dessert is what grand-mothers are for, right? But as your grandchild grows into a teen or young adult, the treats and gifts—and the issues that come with them—get bigger too. What if you have limited retirement income and can't splurge as often as you'd like to? Should you spring for an expensive item that his parents can't afford? Can you give something to one grandchild and not the rest of them? Consider these gift-giving guidelines.

Keep it small. What grandkid wouldn't love having a TV in their bedroom? Well, it's not up to Grandmom. The same goes for video game systems, smartphones, and iPads. Not all parents think these items are good for kids (or kids of a certain age). The cost might not be the issue here—the constant distraction can be a concern—but sometimes it is. Will his parents be annoyed if your grandson loses the $200 sunglasses you bought him? Will *you*? What values are you transmitting when you buy designer sunglasses for a teen anyway? Better to buy him a $10 pair from a kiosk.

Match the gift to the occasion. Birthdays, graduations, bar mitzvahs, confirmations, quinceañeras, sweet sixteens, Eagle Scout ceremonies . . . there's no shortage of milestones that might warrant a big gift. Ask in advance for the child's wish list and if gifting these items is OK. You could be the hero by getting a basketball hoop installed in the driveway—and your grandchild will think of you every time he takes a shot!

Try to keep things equal. Remember when your children were little? Nothing good ever came from saying "Mom likes you best!" But sometimes it's hard not to favor one grandchild, especially if you are closer to one or if one needs more help than others. Try not to show favoritism in your gift giving. If gifts aren't equal in value, they can be equal in number. And don't post on Facebook that you're taking your two oldest granddaughters to the ballet if you're not taking their younger cousins.

Don't buy it; do it. Rather than purchasing something, share an experience with your grandchild, such as a sporting event, Broadway show, concert, beauty appointment, restaurant meal, or even a weekend trip. The happy memories you make can be the greatest gift. (See page 114 for ideas on how to share their interests and hobbies.)

Keep it safe. You might think a skateboard is the perfect gift, but given the number of related injuries, your son or daughter might disagree. Seek parental permission before gifting anything that might be dangerous, sketchy, or controversial. Popular video games and movies often have content that parents disapprove of. The same goes for the fireworks you bought on your road trip, a lesson at the rock climbing gym, or a gift card to the Piercing Pagoda for the belly button ring she wants.

Grandmother Getaways: Trips for the Whole Tribe

Nothing beats having the whole family together. Sure, you could wait for the next wedding (or funeral), but experienced grandparents know that a free vacation is the ultimate draw for full-family fun. Offer your children and grandchildren the chance to join you at a resort or beach and you'll soon be making dinner reservations for twelve. (You don't have to break the bank—props to you if you can pick up the whole tab, but covering just a portion of the bill might entice them to vacation en famille.) These seven family favorites will give you ample opportunity for both togetherness and alone time.

Visit Mickey and friends. Disney is the gold standard of multigenerational vacations. While some family members ride through It's a Small World and relax by the pool, others can brave the Tower of Terror and line up for midnight fireworks. Almost every spot inside the parks is kid-friendly, and many rides and restaurants are accessible for people with limited mobility. You won't have to worry about children misbehaving in a restaurant or not being able to find a convenient bathroom. The downside? Disney is expensive—and crowded. Even the most skilled planners will have to contend with long lines and the high price of park tickets and dining plans. Hit up the internet for money- and time-saving tips from diehard Disney-goers.

Rent a beach or lake house. When you are a crowd, having the run of a whole house with multiple bedrooms and a kitchen for family meals is ideal. People can spread out; some can go tanning and swimming while others ride bikes with the kids. Reserve through a local realtor or use a vacation rental website, like Airbnb.com or VRBO.com, which makes it easy to scout out potential sites and amenities in advance. The most popular beach towns book up many months in advance, so look for fun alternatives on smaller lakes, near rivers, or nestled in mountain ranges (some people even rent out treehouses—hey, why not?).

Sail away. Family cruising is one of the fastest growing segments of the travel industry, and cruise lines offer customized packages for multiple generations traveling together—whether to Alaska, the Bahamas, or the Baltic. As a family, you can scoop up all kinds of amenities, like connecting rooms, family-sized staterooms, abundant dining choices, and private excursions. The boatload of activities to choose from makes it easy to balance personalities, ages, and stamina levels. As one grandmother we spoke to put it, "I only cared that we came together for dinner every night. That's when we heard all the stories about what the kids had been doing all day."

Relax—it's paid for. Mexico, the Caribbean, and the Bahamas are famously home to many all-inclusive beach resorts perfect for honeymoons (or spring break partying), but family-oriented, all-inclusive hotels exist in these locales and throughout the United States, from Colorado to upstate New York. All-inclusive is a great option when traveling with children: you don't have to reach into your wallet every time your grandchild wants a frozen fruit slushie, you never have to risk a meltdown by saying, "No, we're not going on the banana boat ride," and you can split the budget more easily knowing the total cost up front. The one-stop shopping makes vacationing with your extended family, well, *relaxing*.

Saddle up. If your family loves adventure, consider a resort or hotel with a western twang. At your standard dude ranch, horseback riding is the primary attraction, but gorgeous scenery and outdoorsy activities like fishing, cycling, zip-lining, rafting, and archery are also available. If you prefer to chill, you can take a yoga or jewelry-making class. There are evening activities for the family, like campfire sing-alongs and talent contests. Dude ranches abound in the western United States, but you can find some cowboys east of the Mississippi too.

Go Continental. If you want to spend time together and don't mind springing for airfare, consider renting a Tuscan villa, French farmhouse, or other home in the European countryside. You'll get a taste of the food, language, and culture without the hassles that come with navigating a city. Stock your kitchen from the village farmers market, explore the countryside on bicycles, and make friends with the owner of the local ice cream store. Rent a car so the parents can escape for a few hours by themselves. And when your grandkids become teenagers, you can take them to Paris. Maybe you can even leave their parents at home.

Take a family volunteer vacation. Spending quality time together is a fine reason for family travel, but if you want to imbue the trip with a greater purpose, consider "voluntourism." Together with your children and grandchildren you can build a school in Haiti, work in the kitchen on an Israeli army base, or care for sea turtles in Mexico. You can volunteer for a few hours, a few days, or your entire trip. If you prefer to donate goods rather than time on your vacation, check out PackforaPurpose.org. Look up what's needed at your vacation destination so you can pack needed items—everything from toothbrushes to deflated soccer balls and crayons—that you can donate when you arrive.

How to Put Something Away for Their Future

As a grandmother, you naturally want to give your grandchild love, wisdom, interest, and time. But you might also want to give him some of your money. Before you crack open your checkbook, though, seek advice from your accountant or financial planner. How much can you safely give without compromising your retirement income? You might have one grandchild now, but what happens if you have two more? What are the tax advantages, restrictions, and gift rules in your state? Also consult with your son or daughter. How do they feel about your plan? Would they appreciate this help? What are the other grandparents doing? Does that factor into the equation?

If you can, start investing early; thanks to the power of compound interest, a gift today can amount to something significant when they graduate from high school. Besides a tailor-made plan from an expert, here are some of the ways grandparents put money away for their grandkids' future.

A 529 plan. To help families save for future education expenses, many states sponsor qualified tuition plans that give tax-free earnings. You'll choose from a limited set of investment options, and the money can be used for tuition and expenses at elementary, secondary, college, trade, and vocational schools. If you use it for something other than education, you have to pay income tax plus a 10 percent penalty. These plans are generally transferrable to another family member and have only a small impact on the child's financial aid package.

A custodial account. UGMAs and UTMAs, the most common types of such plans, hold assets for the benefit of a minor. You can invest the money any way you wish; earnings are taxed at the child's rate. When your grandchild turns 18 or 21, depending on state laws, he becomes the owner of the account, which means he could use it to pay for a round-the-world backpacking trip instead of education. Colleges consider the money as belonging to the student, which can limit the amount of financial aid offered.

A conceptual college fund. If you prefer a do-it-yourself approach, this type of fund is for you. Open an account with a bank or investment company, earmark it for your grandchild, add money as you wish, and pick whatever mutual or bond funds catch your fancy. When the time comes, you can gift the money to your grandchild—for summer camp, college tuition, or a down payment on a house. If your brood grows, you can divvy up the money among everyone or establish a new account for each child. With all this flexibility come fewer tax benefits; earnings are taxed at your rate, not your grandchild's. And when you do gift the money, you'll have to pay taxes on any amount over the annual gift tax limitation (which was $15,000 in 2018).

A trust fund. Custodial and 529 plans each come with their own regulations, whereas with a trust fund you make the rules. The money need not be transferred at the age of majority; the trust can go on for several generations. You can schedule payouts based on age or milestones, such as when a grandchild buys her first home or graduates from a four-year college with a certain minimum GPA. This flexibility doesn't come cheap; you'll need to hire a lawyer to draw up the trust instrument as well as an administrator to handle the trust's accounting and tax return.

A learning experience. Times have changed since elementary schools had a banking program in which kids could deposit small change into their very own savings account and track the amount in a bank book. But kids still need to learn about money, so along with the gift of money, consider giving your grandchild the gift of your expertise. You could give a share of stock and pair the stock certificate with an age-appropriate book about investing, the company's history, or one of the company's products. Or you could invest together: you provide the seed money and accept the tax liability, and your grandchild can provide the computer know-how and sign you up with an online trading platform like TD Ameritrade or E-Trade. Together, research the companies, track your investments, and decide when to buy and sell (and don't go overboard on your investment amounts—your grandchild isn't a certified financial planner, after all). Later, you can transfer the account into your grandchild's name.

Tips for Sharing Your Memories

What is yesterday's news to you—how you took a trolley to school, bought candy for a penny, and managed with only one phone in your house—can be interesting unknown territory to the younger ones. Sharing stories with your grandchild is a great way to build connections. Consider the following questions when you decide to tell tales about the past.

How will you organize your thoughts?

You can categorize by life cycle events (where you were born, where you went to school, what your wedding was like) or by topic (hobbies, summer activities, favorite books and movies). Or lead with topics that would interest your grandchild, such as sports, pets, music, and what you did for fun when you were his age.

Make a list of questions to keep in front of you to spur your thoughts and guide your stories. These are just a few to get you thinking.

- Where did you grow up?

- What was your house like?

- What did you eat for dinner?

- Did you have siblings?

- Did you watch TV?

- Who was your best friend?

- How did you celebrate holidays and birthdays?

- What songs did your parents sing to you?

Don't worry about putting stories in chronological order. Sometimes the funny incidents or peculiar things that stick out in your mind are the most interesting. Include some stories about your son or daughter, but steer clear of tales about their rebellious teen years (or limit them to the silly and age-appropriate parts). At the end, you will have a priceless and entertaining record of family history to pass on.

How will you record your stories?

You have three basic methods. Ask your grandchild to help you navigate multimedia options.

Writing. Thanks to all that texting and doing homework on the computer, most tweens are pretty good keyboarders. Would your grandchild sit at the computer and type as you dictate? Alternatively, you could sit together and fill a notebook or a special blank "grandparent's memory book," which you can find in any bookstore, and which may include handy features like a blank family tree to fill in, sample questions, and conversation prompts.

Audio. Spoken-word storytelling has been enjoying a resurgence in recent years, thanks to live story slams and the proliferation of podcasts. Could your grandchild record your story on his phone and email the audio file to you? Would you be interested in sharing your personal history with more than just your family? The StoryCorps organization, for instance, has many resources for DIY archivists to record and share widely the stories of ordinary people. Your grandchild could be your collaborator.

Video. Ask your grandchild to film you with a video camera or his smartphone. You don't have to just talk, talk, talk, either—it's a visual medium! Hold up family photos, artwork, or other mementos to preserve them and illustrate your story. Ask for his help with viewing and saving the video on a USB drive, transferring it to a DVD, or uploading it to a video storing and sharing service like Shutterfly.

The Next Generation: How to Embrace Being a Great-Grandmother

You may have *just* become a grandmother, but what's the harm in looking ahead? After all, thanks to increased life expectancy, especially among women, the U.S. Census Bureau has reported a great-grandparent boom. If you're lucky enough to welcome another generation, here's what you can look forward to.

Joy. By the time you become a great-grandmother, you'll be even more keenly aware of how precious time and babies are. On the subject of seeing their great-grandchild for the first time, women we spoke to described a joy that they can barely put into words. But one managed to: "It's a great thrill. Better than the Cyclone roller coaster at Coney Island."

Wonder. Current technology makes it easy to stay in touch with a grandchild. It will be easier a few decades from now, even if your mobility is limited. Who knows what will be possible? You may be able to get to your great-grandchild's house in a self-driving car or on a hyperloop, a train that soars through a vacuum tube nine times faster than a car. With virtual reality you can take a family trip to the Galapagos Islands without getting off the sofa. And when you visit your family, you may not have to offer to help with the dishes; perhaps the robot will do it.

Laughs. Time is elastic for all of us—young and old. It's an especially hard concept for children. So when your great-grandchild comes home from kindergarten and asks if you ever met Ben Franklin, don't be offended. It's hard for him to grasp your lifespan; to him, both the 1700s and the 1900s are a *long* time ago. Instead, just smile, take off your glasses, and tell him how Ben Franklin invented bifocals.

Respect. Let's be honest. If you make it to great-grand-mother status, you deserve credit just for being alive. But you can do a lot more: Pass on cultural traditions and your recipes. Bring family stories to life by showing off your heirlooms. Be a model for aging gracefully. Teach the little ones that family is important. And if you're so inclined, offer your opinion. You've earned it.

Acknowledgments

Thanks to Blair Thornburgh at Quirk Books for remembering that although we aren't yet grandmothers, we know a lot about them. And thanks to all the grandmothers, Bubbes, Nonnas, and Mom-Moms who couldn't wait to share their advice and anecdotes with us. We are grateful to our families, friends, fans, and followers of The Word Mavens—including a lot of those Bubbes—who read our essays, laugh at our book talks, and shmooze with us about family, food, and Jewish traditions.